Remembrance of Meals Past

Remembrance of Meals Past

ANITA LEGSDIN

ReadersMagnet, LLC

Remembrance of Meals Past
Copyright © 2019 by Anita Legsdin

Published in the United States of America
ISBN Paperback: 978-1-950947-72-0
ISBN eBook: 978-1-950947-73-7

All rights reserved. No part of this publication may be reproduced, stored in a retrieval system or transmitted in any way by any means, electronic, mechanical, photocopy, recording or otherwise without the prior permission of the author except as provided by USA copyright law.

The opinions expressed by the author are not necessarily those of ReadersMagnet, LLC.

ReadersMagnet, LLC
10620 Treena Street, Suite 230 | San Diego, California, 92131 USA
1.619.354.2643 | www.readersmagnet.com

Book design copyright © 2019 by ReadersMagnet, LLC. All rights reserved.
Cover design by Ericka Walker
Interior design by Shemaryl Evans

Contents

Introduction 7
The Cheesecake Wars 9
The Paella Prototype 14
Blind Date 19
A Good Year for Apples 24
Ladies of the Night 29
Conversations with the Dead 32
Culinary Divorce or, the Souring of a Relationship ... 43
Comfort Foods and Cravings 47
Meatloaf Afternoon 54
The Sins of the Fathers 58
Recipes 63
    Cheesecake 64
    Paella 65
    Pasta 67
    Sautéed Boletus 68
    Dough for Latvian Sheet Bread 69
    Apple Sheet Bread 70
    Latvian Cheesecake 71
    Paskha (Russian Easter Dessert) 72
    Leg of Lamb 74
    Latvian Sauerkraut 75
    Meatloaf 76
    Shepherd's Pie 77

Introduction

It isn't only Marcel Proust who associates vivid memories with certain foods. We all know people who can tell stories of Aunt Zelda, who sends a particular fruitcake each Christmas, or cousin Lottie, who boils all her vegetables until they are completely dead.

The stories in this collection, with a few exceptions, all are based on events from my life. Names have been changed, and fictional events added, to conceal and protect identities. The story *Conversations With the Dead* is, of course, sheer fantasy, as is most of *Sins of the Fathers*. All others have at least a grain of truth in them, which served as inspiration.

The background information presented in *The Cheesecake Wars* is true. My mother's mother did have French ancestry, and did learn to cook in France. She was the head chef for Pavlova, the Russian ballerina.

These stories were all written at different times, without the idea of gathering them into a collection. Because of this, you may see some repetition.

—Anita Legsdin

The Cheesecake Wars

I HOLD IN MY HAND MY mother's little black book of favorite recipes, looking for inspiration. The book is a collection of successes, dishes that, from experience, she learned everyone loved. I can taste every page. This one is Sunday evening, when the menu always consisted of soup, fish, cheese, and tea. It's taken me a long time to appreciate soup, but I still don't like fish, cheese or tea. I'm not quite sure why.

My mother raised me on stories about her mother, who learned to cook in France (she had French ancestry), and who became head chef for a Russian ballerina. I yearned for a different universe, one in which I could have known this marvelous woman who was my mother's mother, touched her romantic life, learned from her how to cook and how to tell fortunes with cards. But I had to make do with my mother's stories, which usually consisted of diatribes about how little time my grandmother gave to her family, and how it wasn't until my mother's wedding day that she received her first crash course in cooking. Oh, the hassle of having a professional chef for a mother!

It wasn't until I reached adulthood, left home and began to cook on my own that I began to realize my mother wasn't the best cook in America. The cheesecake incident was one of my first disillusionments; it started one of the first battles between me and my mother. In fact, cheesecake has been the subject of several wars in my life.

I don't remember when I was first introduced to cheesecake. In my family, we only ate sweets on special holidays such as Easter, when my mother made *Paskha* and *Kulich*, two of her Russian specialties; desserts I dearly loved. Her recipes for them are in this little black book. When I met Lori in college, whose mother made the best cheesecake west of the Mississippi, it was a novelty to me.

Lori's mother's recipe was the first cheesecake I knew. Lori would bring the cheesecake to all the potluck lunches or dinners held by the club we both belonged to. I got the recipe from her, it is deceptively simple, and I still use it to this day. It's here in my mother's little black book, entitled "Mother McKenzie's cheesecake," the pages in my handwriting. I am puzzled: why did my mother have the recipe, since she never made it? And how did it come to be in my handwriting? She must have asked for it once.

Mrs. McKenzie, Lori's mother, majored in home economics in college. Lori and I both looked up to her as knowing how to set a perfect table, how to plan meals, how to be a gracious hostess. A stark contrast to my mother, an immigrant who wasn't familiar with the customs of this new country, and who couldn't teach me how to become comfortable with American ways. Mrs. McKenzie's cheesecake symbolized a departure from my immigrant past, an attempt to assimilate myself into my new nationality.

When I graduated college and proudly entered the working world, I was introduced to the custom of monthly birthday lunches. I worked at a small office—fewer than fifty employees—and once a month someone brought in a treat to honor those who had birthdays that month. In those days, of course, it was the women of the office who bore the responsibility for bringing the treats. Some women managed to get away with bringing cakes, cookies or donuts they bought rather than made themselves, but that was generally frowned upon. I, too, succumbed to the tacit competition, wanting to be one of those blessed with many requests for the recipe. After all, I had to live up to my grandmother's sterling example.

When my turn came to cook, I prepared cheesecake, of course. We celebrated only one birthday that month. It happened to be Edna's, the oldest employee, five years from retirement. Being one who always respects age, I wanted to impress Edna with my

Remembrance of Meals Past

culinary skill. The time for coffee break came. Everyone was called into the lunchroom, where I unveiled my masterpiece.

Edna peered through her glasses, then nodded. "Oh, good. I was hoping you wouldn't bring anything I'd have to break my diet for. No offense, but I hate cheesecake." And she promptly walked out of her own birthday party. It didn't matter to me that nearly every woman there asked me for the recipe. It didn't matter to me that the cheesecake was so popular there was hardly a piece left for me. Edna, the one I'd prepared it for, had refused to eat it.

Had I been ten years older, I could have shrugged off the incident. Had I been twenty years older, I might have known to ask Edna what she liked rather than presenting her with my own favorite dish. But, being then in my early twenties and still naïve, I was crushed. I decided that Edna just didn't know how to appreciate the finer things in life.

It wasn't until I got engaged that the battle with my mother began.

Rick and I went through the usual rituals of introducing one another to our respective families. In contrast to my family, which consisted of just me and my mother, his was quite large: both parents, two brothers, several aunts, uncles, and countless cousins. The first time my mother met Rick, she insulted him grandly. He had a beard, which to her indicated he was unwashed, unkempt. (It didn't occur to me to remind her that her beloved father sported a mustache and beard all his life.) She piled insult upon insult, embarrassing me and offending Rick. From their first meeting, he hated my mother, and never forgave her afterwards. It wasn't until much later that I understood this was the old European manner, my mother's way of checking to see if he was serious about me and worthy of my affection. Even though he might have passed her test, it was at the cost of losing a son-in-law's affection and respect.

Now that I was the mistress of my own (small) household, I invited my mother to my house to share dinner with me and my new husband. I served the best meal I could think of: leg of lamb, always my father's favorite, with fresh vegetables, and, of course, Mrs. McKenzie's cheesecake for dessert.

Rick's love of cooking was one of his traits that endeared him to me the most. He appreciated my skill in the kitchen, and we both enjoyed fixing and eating gourmet meals. We both agreed that his British grandmother grew peas on the vine until they were near-dead, then boiled them until they lost their identity. The same was true for meats: except for turkey, all were boiled, cooked until you no longer needed a knife to eat them. In contrast, the vegetables Rick and I prepared for my mother still retained their fresh flavor, and the lamb was baked in the manner of Julia Child: still pink in the middle. I believed my grandmother would have been proud—at least, I hoped so.

I was too young then to understand my mother's need to be my mentor. Whereas I sought independence and my own life, she yearned to give me advice and counsel, advice her stubborn daughter rarely asked for. What choice did she have but to criticize this meal she had no part in preparing? The lamb was not done, she declared. The vegetables were undercooked. And by the time we got to the cheesecake, she had no room for it.

She took one petite bite. "Too rich for me," she declared, pushing away the plate and pouting. "Bring me some coffee."

Eventually, my mother returned the favor and invited both Rick and me to dinner at her apartment. I can't remember the first meal she fixed for us, but the vegetables had started out frozen, and were boiled in a manner that would have pleased Rick's British grandmother. Dessert, surprisingly, was cheesecake: instant cheesecake from a box. She even showed me the box, proudly. "See," she declared. "How easy. And it contains much less fat than yours. It's much lighter."

My mother is not subtle. For at least a year afterwards, every meal I had at her house ended with that cheesecake in a box. Mother rarely lived cheesecake before then; in fact, I could not remember her ever having fixed it before. Now, to find it consistently the dessert of choice was confusing, unnerving. Why was she rubbing it in, and what exactly was the lesson I was supposed to learn? I never talked about the cheesecake, rarely ate any, and eventually

Remembrance of Meals Past

she stopped serving it. Men wage wars with guns, missiles, and bombs. Women wage wars at home, with food. Somebody won and somebody lost here, but I'm not sure who. Perhaps my mother and I both lost.

I still occasionally make the cheesecake when I have the rare craving for it. It's simple and far lighter than other, denser cheesecakes. Neither I nor my friends can tolerate rich desserts anymore, and unfortunately, I can now understand Edna's refusal to eat it. Much as I'd like to, I can no longer hold a grudge against her. Besides, these days, chocolate desserts such as Death By Chocolate or Chocolate Decadence are far more popular. Nevertheless, I retain a fondness for the simple yet elegant cheesecake made by my friend's mother, which symbolizes my youth, and my first American dessert.

The little black recipe book contains my mother's victories. They are foods everyone loved, or recipes gathered from friends who had cooked other tasty, successful dishes. I finally came to understand how difficult it was for my mother to feel competent in the kitchen. She always followed a recipe faithfully, never wavering from quantities or substituting ingredients. And having experienced firsthand the consequences of having a mother who was too busy to share her cooking skills, my mother probably didn't want me to experience the same thing. It's one of her most precious legacies to me, her legacy of nurturing, comfort, and warm, fulfilling memories.

Too bad about the cheesecake.

The Paella Prototype

NO MEAL IS EVER AS TASTY as the one you never ate. Imagination does wonders. When Sylvia and her mother would go to the movies when she was small, Sylvia would close her eyes during the scary parts. "Don't bother closing your eyes," her mother would say. "What you imagine, from the soundtrack, will always be worse than what's actually on the screen."

But then, those were the days before special effects grew to maturity. Sylvia's mother probably could never have imagined "Friday the 13th" or "Texas Chainsaw Massacre." Also, her mother survived five years of World War II Germany as a refugee, so she probably saw far worse than Sylvia ever would. But her remarks about the power of imagination were right on the mark.

The paella incident proved to Sylvia, at age twenty-six, that reality could never match the illusion she built from of visions of splendor, immortality, and undying love. She'd never heard of paella before. Guy and his friend Sam introduced the dish to her, which was to become her nemesis.

It's supposed to be a good sign that you and the person you're involved with enjoying one another's friends. Sylvia and Guy had been going together for six months and were now beginning the dance of showing one another off to their friends. Sylvia fell in love with Sam and his house when she first met him. She was glad Guy was introducing her to his friends, and she was glad she liked Sam; a good sign of things to come. She studiously forgot Guy's constant criticisms of her friends: "they're all dykes," he declared.

Remembrance of Meals Past

"But I've known them all my life," she replied, "we have fun together."

"I'll bet," he answered.

The Mount Baker district in Seattle is a mélange of rich and poor, a hilly area where vacant lots and spectacular views abound. Lots are vacant because, for the most part, they are unbuildable. Sam lived above one of those vacant lots. His house looked unremarkable from the street, but once you were inside, you realized the drab simplicity was a front, that you had to be inside to appreciate its true character. If Sylvia were to build a house to express her character, she would do the same. She saw herself in the same words she used to describe the house: you had to get to know her to really appreciate her. She didn't cast her pearls before swine.

The house had ceilings well over eight feet high. Each room was sparsely populated, with well-chosen, obviously expensive furniture whenever there was furniture. Sam had plants, large and healthy ones as opposed to Sylvia's small, struggling ones. His favorite room (and hers as well) was the music room, which faced the cliff behind the house. It overlooked a forest of maple and evergreens, with Lake Washington shimmering beyond the treetops. Because of the angle of the hillside, you could hardly see more than two or three houses. The room was empty but for a mahogany baby grand, a palm tree, which stood well over six feet tall, and large soft pillows scattered in various corners. Guy stood with his arm around her shoulder, listening is Sam's studied singer's voice murmured in the background. Later, Sylvia realized she did more gazing out the window than conversing with Guy and his friend Sam. She only realized much later that she was the only woman there.

Sam himself was a person she would like to have had as a friend. Overweight just enough to be called well-fed, affluent enough to afford to be benevolent to the world, he had a wonderful sense of humor and a quick mind. After observing Sylvia for less than ten minutes, he was able to tell her how she entertained herself, and that her silences were reticent rather than bashful. She liked people who weren't fooled by her appearance. She thought she and Sam hit it off faster than she and Guy ever did. Too bad about the paella.

"Sam's going to be singing at the Mark Tobey on Friday nights," Guy said when he phoned. "He's throwing a party to celebrate. It's going to be great, he's fixing something really special. Sam's a great cook. What are you doing Saturday?"

Sylvia beamed. As Guy described the party, she imagined Sam's house, with Guy and her in it, eating this very special dish his friend Sam would be cooking. "I haven't made any plans yet, I could come."

There was a brief silence. "Oh. Well, I don't know how to say this without making you mad. I knew I shouldn't have told you. I don't want to make you mad at me or at Sam. Sam asked me to tell you he doesn't have anything against you personally, but," he sighed, "you're not invited."

"*What?*"

"See, what'd I tell you? Now you're mad."

"Of course I'm mad. What did you have to go tell me about the party for, if I'm not invited?"

"It's just that he's going to be serving something special. It's going to be a real treat, and it costs a lot of money, and he wants it to go around. The recipe only feeds so many, you know. You cook, too, you ought to know. There just won't be enough to go around if more people start showing up."

There was another silence. Sylvia knew he wanted her to say she understood. She didn't.

He went on. "Honest, I wanted you to come, Sam would've invited you, but there just won't be enough to go around. I'm sorry. Now you're mad."

She was more than mad, she was disgusted. Sam, who she'd thought to be kind, benevolent and jolly, was conspiring with Guy against her. She wanted to change the subject, but didn't know what to say. "What's he going to be serving that's so special, that costs so much?"

"It's called paella. I don't know what's in it, but it's got lots of stuff in it, good stuff."

Good stuff. Hmph.

The paella was the first of many incidents that strained their relationship to the breaking point. Guy always told Sylvia she was a masochist; she decided she was, because after that fateful Saturday, she couldn't stop herself from asking about the paella. He described it to her in painful detail: Saffron rice, tiny bits of chicken and sausage; delicate spices, abundant piles of seafood. She saw Sam's house, the music room facing water and gently swaying treetops, someone playing the piano and Sam singing in his crooning jazz voice. She saw the bare hardwood floors, the pristine white walls, the palm tree. And, she saw the paella.

How do you describe a flavor? The only thing Sylvia knew about saffron was that it was yellow. Curry was yellow, too—did the taste of saffron resemble curry? She tried to imagine piles of seafood and sausage, some of her favorite foods, and her mouth began to water.

She never asked Guy who else was at the party, or even how many people came. He never volunteered the information, either. They never went to visit Sam again.

Later, after they broke up, her curiosity finally drove her to experience the dish herself. She carefully chose the company and the restaurant, to guarantee she would have a good time. She went to one of the new Spanish restaurants in Pioneer Square, a district full of artists and craftsmen, the Seattle equivalent of Soho, with her childhood friend Marie, the one whom Guy had called cruel names. A pair of musicians hovered over their table, playing lovely Spanish guitar music. They drank a lot of wine and had great fun. The paella was indeed a good dish, but not as delectable as the meal in her mind, the one she had never tasted.

It was Marie who broke the news to Sylvia sometime later. "You remember Guy, who you used to go out with?"

"How could I forget?"

Marie leaned toward Sylvia, dropping her voice to a whisper. "He's moved to San Francisco. He's living with someone called

Sam." She raised one eyebrow, as only Marie can do. "Did you have any idea he was gay?"

Several years later, one of her friends married. They celebrated the event at a friend's house, another memorable house: an enormous Victorian mansion in the manner Sylvia herself would like to live. But by then, her tastes had changed. Bare hardwood floors had been replaced by oriental carpets, sparse designer furniture by plentiful antiques. The reception was potluck. She brought a chocolate cheesecake with raspberry sauce; the hostess served a tureen of gazpacho, someone else brought a salad with nasturtium leaves and rose petals. The cousin of the bride brought in a huge casserole, unveiling a steaming mound of assorted meats atop yellow rice. Someone standing next to Sylvia asked what it was. "Paella," the cousin responded.

"Oh, have some," added the bride, "she makes *wonderful* paella!" She turned to Sylvia, pushing her toward the dish. "Go. Have some before it's all gone. You have to have some. It's the best paella I've ever tasted."

It was indeed good paella, but somehow not quite the way Sylvia imagined it should be. She loved paella. But she hated it.

Blind Date

It was Ron, my friend Debbie's husband, who set me up with Patrick. And yes, I do mean "set me up" in all of its meanings. Given Ron's history, I should have been suspicious, but I thought, *what the hey, I'll just roll with it.*

"There's a friend of mine I think you should get to know," Ron said. "His name's Pat, and I gave him your phone number. He's a cool guy."

My first reaction was shock; he gave out my phone number to a stranger, without my permission? But I didn't say anything. Ron is like that, and anything I'd say wouldn't make a difference. Take it as an adventure. There were currently no men in my life, maybe this would work out OK. We did, after all, both have a common friend in Ron.

I got the phone call the next day.

"Hi, this is Patrick. I hope you don't mind. Ron gave me your phone number."

"That's OK, Pat. I'm an adult, I can handle it."

"Umm ...my friends call me Patrick."

"Oh, sorry—Patrick." I could have sworn Ron referred to him as Pat. But he probably did that on purpose, just for laughs.

We talked for a short while. Turns out he was a bus driver, liked foreign movies just like I do. He suggested we meet at his place on the weekend, take a walk if the weather was nice. If not, we could go down to the aquarium on the waterfront.

He lived in a relatively new apartment building at the foot of Magnolia hill, with an unobstructed view of the railroad switching yards across the street. "The trains sit with their engines all night," he said, "but so far it's just background white noise. Come on, I thought we could go down to Discovery Park, it's nice there."

Patrick turned out to be shorter than I'd imagined. To tell the truth, I wasn't sure what I imagined—a clone of Ron, maybe? He was small and thin, shorter than me. But then I'm 5'9", and a lot of men are shorter than me.

He suggested we take the bus. "I can go anywhere free, I have a pass because I'm a bus driver."

"I can drive, I don't mind," I said. "My car's just over there."

He shook his head. "No sense wasting gas. Come on, the bus stop is just over there, and there should be a bus coming real soon. We can take it to the end of the line and go from there."

One of my biggest faults is that I don't put my foot down often enough, or with enough force. "OK," I said. "I'll let someone else drive." I decided not to point out that the so-called wasted gas was probably equivalent to the cost of the ticket I had to buy.

It turned out Patrick didn't even own a car, he took the bus everywhere he went in Seattle.

"But what happens if you want to take a trip to the ocean or to Portland or Bellingham," I asked.

"Well, there are trains to Portland and Bellingham," he answered. "As for other places. I try to find someone else who's going there, or else I hitchhike."

"Eek. isn't that dangerous?"

He laughed, a high-pitched somewhat shrill giggle. "For a woman, probably. But I've never had a problem."

On the way, we passed a small restaurant that specialized in pizza. I pointed to it. "Is that place any good?"

He shrugged. "I don't know, I never eat out."

"Oh, really?"

"Waste of money. Plus, you never know what you're getting, or how many chemicals are in it. Just walking past it makes me sick. Smell that grease!"

I sniffed, but didn't detect a smell any different than other restaurants. Maybe I just wasn't sensitive enough.

The rest of the afternoon went pretty well. He knew the bus driver who took us to the park, of course, and they talked shop all the way over. I was glad this first "date," if that's what it was, was something different than the usual meeting in a bar or café. I appreciate people who enjoy the fresh air and walking.

We got off at the end of the line and headed toward the park, which was only a few blocks away. The Magnolia district is fairly rich, and I enjoyed looking at the large homes as we passed them. But Patrick turned out to be just as much of a reverse snob as Ron was. He thought people who lived in large homes were ostentatious. Large homes were a waste of space and money. I let him rant and didn't say much.

We walked for a good hour, mostly around the perimeter of the bluff overlooking the water. We didn't see any eagles, although Patrick said there were some nesting in the area, and he'd seen them occasionally.

We went back to the same bus stop where we'd gotten off; there was a bus already there, waiting for its scheduled departure time. "Well," I said as we sat down.

"That's a deep subject," Patrick answered, letting loose his high-pitched giggle again. "That raised a pretty good appetite in me. How about I fix us dinner?"

I hesitated for a moment, then agreed. He seemed to think he was a good cook, and I was indeed getting hungry, not to mention thirsty. OK, let's see what this guy can do.

Back at his apartment, he gave me a cup of herb tea and suggested we sit on the balcony for a while. Just in front of the balcony was a small green area.

Patrick pointed. "There's a house pretty much next door to this, but the trees hide it. I like it because it's almost like being in the woods."

"Except for the sound of the trains coupling," I said, smiling.

"I like that sound, for some reason," he said. "But I have to admit it's annoying when my neighbors get noisy. I make sure I tell the manager whenever they get too loud."

The rest of the conversation depressed me. I noticed he didn't seem to have a television, and asked why.

"Too much mindless junk," he answered.

"Yeah, you can watch a lot of shows on the computer, pick and choose what you want to watch."

He giggled again. "Computer? What computer? More mindless junk. A waste of electricity."

"But there's a lot you can do with computers that make life easier, like filing taxes online, or paying bills."

"One word: hackers. Besides, what's wrong with pencil and paper? I prefer to support the postal system, I pay my bills the old-fashioned way."

I asked him what he did for fun.

"Walking. Reading."

I asked what he liked to read, and he answered, "Science fiction. They're the only intelligent books around."

"Sounds like you'd do well living on a farm."

He nodded. "That's what I'm saving up for. A log cabin, somewhere maybe in Montana or Idaho. I think I'd like that." He looked around. "Well, I think it's time for me to get into the kitchen. Give me a few minutes."

I wondered whether or not I wanted to continue being Patrick's friend. I felt no chemistry and too much negativity. Although I thought it unfair to say he was too short for me (but I'm sure my mother would have said that), he compounded that deficiency by his strange sense of humor and that giggle of his. But what else could I expect from a friend of Ron's? So, let's see what he fixes for dinner, maybe there's a future there.

A short while later, he came out and called me to come and eat. The table was nicely set. He went into the kitchen and came back out, carrying a huge bowl piled high with an enormous quantity of what looked like spaghetti. "Don't you just *love* pasta," he exclaimed.

"Uh, I don't eat it that much," I mumbled.

He set down the bowl. I looked at it; that's what it was, just pasta. No sauce. I remembered reading columns in the *Times* written by a restaurant critic, whose favorite refrain was, "not enough sauce."

"It's tossed with butter," he said, "this is the way they eat pasta in Italy."

Never having been to Italy, I couldn't answer, although I suspected that at least the Italians would have sprinkled a bit of cheese on top of the noodles. A survey of the table revealed no cheese. No salad. Nothing but the plain noodles tossed with butter.

Patrick went back into the kitchen and returned with a tall glass of milk. When he asked me what I wanted to drink, I said I'd just have the tea, thanks. I nibbled at my spaghetti while Patrick dug into it wholeheartedly, slurping noisily. The pasta was OK—just OK—with the butter, but I'd hoped for something less bland. Even garlic bread would have been good.

It was after that first date that I called the phone company and asked for a caller ID so that I could decline to answer the phone if Patrick called again. He did call a few times, but I made up excuses not to see him, and he eventually gave up.

I have refused to eat pasta ever since.

A Good Year for Apples

JANIS SITS IN THE CHAIR LIKE an adult sitting in a doll's house. He speaks slowly, in a quiet voice. "The weather is unusually warm for October. It usually rains, dismal weather." He pauses. "It was also like this during the war, I remember. Nineteen forty-two, the year the Russians took Riga. October 13. We were in the country then, entire families taking refuge in the woods, with all our horses, cows and dogs." He nods. "It was warm then, too, like it is now." I feel the dark shadow of his memories pass over me. He relates how they were discovered when one of the dogs began barking at a squirrel. How do you prevent a dog from barking?

Janis is married to my cousin Sonja, the daughter of my father's brother. He must be nearly seven feet tall, and in the mid-1950s he was on the Latvian championship basketball team. Because of his athlete status, the Communists spared him from deportation to Siberia. He had relative freedom of movement while the team traveled throughout free Europe, a rare blessing for a citizen of the then-Soviet state of Latvia.

We are sitting at the dining room table in their small Riga apartment. In the United States, it would be called a one-bedroom apartment. In Latvia, it is called a three-room apartment. Each room, not counting the kitchen or bathroom, was considered a potential sleeping area by the Soviet government. During Communist times, this apartment housed Sonja, her husband Janis, their daughter Rita and her husband. Rita's two small children, and a native Russian stranger. And this family was considered lucky—other families had to share similar apartments with even more strangers.

Remembrance of Meals Past

I am a first-generation refugee, born in a Displaced Persons camp in Germany after the end of WWII. My parents had spent five years there, after fleeing the Communist invasion of Latvia. Latvians hated both the Communists and Nazis, but lacked sufficient resources to fight both those powerful countries. Both my mother and father died before Latvia, Lithuania, and Estonia regained their freedom; I always wonder how they would have reacted to that news. Would they have moved back?

My father would have been pleased to know that I finally have re-established contact with his family. When I graduated from college, he gave me my cousin's name and address, and a recent photo. "Here. This is your cousin, my brother's daughter. You need to have relations with your family. Write to her."

Bewildered at the short introduction. I replied, "OK, Dad."

What does an adolescent say to a total stranger? Especially to one who is nearly twenty years older and does not speak English. I wrote polite, short letters that my mother helped me translate. But over the years, my enthusiasm waned. I married, changed names, moved, and lost contact with the Seattle Latvian community. Eventually, the letters stopped, but I never lost the guilt. Here I was, enjoying the freedom and earning a good living, while my blood relatives lived in oppression and poverty half a world away.

When my mother died, all my hope for a translator disappeared. Although Latvian was my first language and I understand and speak it, I never learned to write it. It took blood, sweat, tears, and eight full hours to produce a few short paragraphs full of mistakes. Whenever I wrote to my aunt in Chicago, she sent the letters back to me, corrections marked in red pencil. With that kind of encouragement, I soon began writing to her in English. What would my Latvian relatives think of me if I sent letters that were obviously written by a near-illiterate? I could imagine them clucking their tongues, saying, "Didn't her parents teach her any respect for her native tongue?" But the reality is that they'd be glad to hear from me, no matter what language I wrote in. The guilt and intimidation are all in my mind.

The liberation of the Baltic countries sparked a renewed interest in me to try and find my cousin once again. But many questions still remained: did she still not know English? Did she have access to a translator? Did she live in the same place any more? Was she even alive? Although I spent many agonized hours thinking about sending another letter, I never did.

The year was 1992. Out of the blue, a letter arrived from Chicago. The return address showed a Latvian name, but one I did not know. Who would be writing to me from Chicago, and why? When I opened the letter, I was overwhelmed. My cousin Sonja was in the United States, visiting; she had even been in Seattle to look for me, but it wasn't until she arrived in Chicago that she found someone who knew where I was living. The circle was, once again, complete.

I managed to phone Sonja before she returned to Latvia. Excited about the prospect of actually meeting her, I arranged for a short ten-day visit, saving a longer visit for another year.

The brief visit the following year is full of activity. We go everywhere, see everybody. As poor as they are, everyone gives me a gift to bring home as a souvenir. I have more relatives here, both distant and close, than I do in America, it seems. I even meet a distant cousin with the same name as mine! Although I am ashamed I do not speak the language better, I slip easily back into my childhood language. Even though my speech is full of errors, everyone forgives me. At last, I am here.

When I was little, my mother had a bag full of dried mushrooms she used for special occasions: "*Tie ir isti Baravikas,*" she said – they are real *Baravikas* from Latvia. They were the most delicious mushrooms I had tasted—meaty, substantial. Eventually, the bag was used up, and we never got more, but I never forgot the rich, deep flavor that tasted almost like roast beef. Of course, no one knew the English equivalent for *Baravikas*. Rumor had it that we had some in Washington State, but we did not know where, and both my parents were afraid of picking something that looked similar but was actually deadly poison. "Don't fool around with mushrooms," my mother always said. "They may look pretty, but looks can fool you."

It is late September in Latvia, high season for mushrooms. Take any train that goes out to the country, and you find people leaving in the morning with empty baskets and returning in the afternoon with full ones for dinner: *Bekas* and *Baravikas*, the most delicious mushrooms imaginable, free for the taking. Finally, I would be able to find out what they really were.

Forests in Latvia are mostly pine and birch, with little or no underbrush. Latvians are proud of their clean forests, unlike the "dirty forests" of Russia that have so much undergrowth you cannot walk through them. I do not tell Sonja about the forests in Washington State, which surely must resemble those dense, despised Russian forests. Sonja points to large shrubs growing along the roadside, similar to Scotch broom. She snorts. "The *Russians* brought those. We didn't have any before they invaded."

My cousin has a sixth sense for mushrooms. Or maybe it's just because she's been picking them since she was a little girl. We locate a spot she knows must have many, but which is not overrun with other mushroom hunters. Looking down, I see the ground full, mushrooms everywhere. "What's this one?" I ask.

She waves her hand. "That's nothing. Those have no flavor, they're not worth the trouble."

We continue on, I at a snail's pace, examining every brown and white patch I see, but Sonja strides through the woods like a race-walker trying to reach the front of the pack. This is mushroom hunting? I am used to looking for Chanterelles, crawling along in tiny steps, peeking under every leaf. But here, there are no fallen leaves from broadleaf trees, only pine needles, and mushrooms. Sonja suddenly stops and bends down. She has found some. At the end of an hour, her basket is full, and I have found only the inedible or poisonous ones. She has had many more years of practice than I.

Back at her daughter's home, Sonja and I clean and chop the mushrooms we collected, as well as the ones Rita and her two sons picked. It is a huge pile. We will have some for dinner tonight, as an accompaniment to potatoes, and she will prepare some to preserve for a longer time. Even though I am impressed by the collection, Sonja tells me it is not a good year for mushrooms. The autumn weather is too warm, too dry. It is a better year for apples.

I photograph our collected pile of mushrooms, and sketch them as best I can. Sonja knows German also, and tells me the German name for the mushrooms: they are *Steinpilz*, she tells me.

Aha! German dictionaries abound in America; surely I can find what they are. After I return home, I discover that both *Bekas* and *Baravikas* are of the *Boletus* variety, and yes indeed, they grow in my home state. I make a note to try and find good locations where *Boletus* grow.

The visit is too short. I collect names, addresses and phone numbers, and promise to write. They even tell me I can write in English, because Sonja has been taking lessons, and her grandsons are learning English in school. Sonja gives me some old photographs of my father when he was small, together with his three brothers. We all cry when I leave, but I know I will come back again. The connection will never be lost.

After coming home, I resume my normal activity. The first week, I bask in the warm memories of being surrounded by the language I grew up with, and of being called by the nickname only my parents used. I go for a walk by the shores of the lake near my home, feeling like a child again. I see a pine tree not far away, in a small city park. I had not particularly noticed it before, but I see it clearly now. Fir trees abound here, but pines at this altitude are more rare. I walk up closer to it, remembering the vast pine forests of Latvia where you could see clearly for such great distances.

As I approach the tree, I see shapes, lumps coming out of the ground underneath it. I bend over to take a closer look – they are *Baravikas*! Not many, about four, but they are *isti Baravikas*. In my home town, not a mile from my house. It is a message from the other side of the world; tears fill my yes. I maybe thousands of miles away from my family, but we are still connected.

Ladies of the Night

It's been a long time since I've had any contact with the Latvian community—my ancestral heritage. I decide to join the group of women who do crafts; it's a chance to make friends, if possible, and definitely gives me the chance to speak Latvian again (as if I'd ever forget my native language).

They meet in a basement room of the Latvian church. We arrive at seven in the evening. There are at least five or six of us who all come at once, punctually at seven, descending the stairs in an orderly line. Latvians are always punctual and orderly. We file into the room; everyone pulls up a chair to the long table. I introduce myself as a new member of their group. "Let's see," a woman says, "where will you sit?" She addresses each chair by the name of its usual occupant, trying to fit in one extra.

It turns out everyone actually *does* have an assigned seat. I am seated next to Andra Kaukuls; since we are "related," I must sit next to her, at least on the first day. I feel like I've been thrown into 18th century England. This is a set for "Pride and Prejudice," isn't it?

A box full of teddy bears sits in the middle of the table. Identical teddy bears, all of them wearing the same grin, all of them staring out of identical eyes. "Teddy bears sell well," one woman explains. They are all destined for the November holiday bazaar (and this is still January).

Andra Kaukuls arrives; she and I are both cousins of the same woman who still lives in Latvia: Andra related from her mother's side, I from her father's. In English the relationship sounds far less complex than the way Andra originally explained it to me. This is because the word for "uncle" is either "father's brother" or "mother's brother," depending on the relationship. The relationship in Latvian, therefore, becomes "my father's sister married her mother's brother." (Huh?) I am certain this is why the Latvian culture has survived so long, through so many foreign occupations: any brain that can untie the knots of a sentence like Andra's cannot help but maintain superiority over simple beings with simple languages.

Andra has brought two projects, so she works on one and I on the other. This is a social occasion, a true quilting bee. Someone has just returned from a cruise, and has brought pictures; half the group has gathered around her to look at the photos. Another woman is surrounded by flowers: it's her birthday, and later we sing to her.

Andra, the cousin of my cousin, introduces me to a whole other dimension: the second room, where "the white ladies" work. These women (there are only four or five) work with handlooms, weaving traditional headbands and belts for national costumes. They seriously ponder pictures showing costumes from different regions, for a national costume must be authentic to the smallest detail. A white skirt is spread out on one of the tables, a lightweight wool daintily gathered at the waist, one of the woven bands stitched to the waistband.

The designs the other women are studying will decorate the hemline. I'm afraid to touch it for fear of leaving behind fingerprints. They also embroider tablecloths and napkins for these white ladies. For tonight, though, I will sit with the other women, the "*raibas damns*" (speckled women); the word "*raibas*" means both "speckled" and "of mixed origin." We are the ladies of the night, the "*Vakaretajas*." ("*Vakars*" is Latvian for evening; "*Vakaretajas*" simply means "women who meet in the evening.") It's one of the most powerful and respected groups of the local Latvian community, consisting mostly of the original generation of immigrants.

At one point (I don't know when, since I'm not wearing a watch), one of them stands up. She rings a bell she has brought. It's time to make announcements, and everyone stops their work to listen. I am introduced as a new member, and all of them introduce themselves. Most I already know, they already were pillars of the community when I was a child. They speak the language of my childhood, and I am the youngest there. I do feel like a child again, speaking the

Remembrance of Meals Past

language spoken by my parents, both of whom are deceased. We sing the traditional birthday song to the one who is surrounded by flowers, and then it's time to eat.

At one end of the room stands a buffet table, piled high with food, foods I was accustomed to eating when I was growing up, and which I haven't had, mostly, in a long time: *piragi* (the traditional stuffed rolls served at every occasion); open-faced sandwiches with sliced ham or slices of cucumber, each topped with one shrimp; apple sheet bread, several different kinds of sweet yellow bread containing cardamon, raisins, nuts and some candied fruit, twisted into a gigantic braid; grapes; mandarin oranges that have been peeled and sectioned; coffee, and tea. They are all as perfect as they would have been had this been a formal occasion. I rarely cook any of these for myself, and the buffet spread reminds me of all the holidays spent with my parents and their friends.

At first we all stand in line, taking a paper plate as we arrived at the table, loading our plate with what we want. Later, as we've eaten most of it, two women pass platters around to us, encouraging us to help ourselves to seconds and thirds. Such a feast!

We continue working and talking after the meal is over. Andra inspects my work, telling me where my stitches are too loose or too tight. I rip out a section and do it over until she is satisfied. It's a baby blanket, with a simple shell pattern in pink and white. I still have to prove I know how to crochet, even though I've been doing it most of my life.

Precisely at nine o'clock, the woman with the bell stands up and announces the evening is over, it's time to go home. Those who baked the bread and made the sandwiches distribute the leftovers, urging us to take some for the trip home or the next day. All of us pack up our things in an orderly manner, and leave. The next meeting is in two weeks. Rita Zommers, the wife of one of our wealthier members, who lives in a multimillion-dollar home overlooking the bay, leans over me and says "I hope we didn't offend you, and that this won't be your last time." I laugh and say I'll be back. And I will.

Driving home, I can't help smiling all the way. I feel like I've finally been fed.

Conversations with the Dead

Martin filled his friends' glasses for the third time, but the bottle remained far from empty, when he set it down on the small table, it appeared more full than when he'd begun pouring.

"Moselle?" asked George Benson. Unlike the other two old men seated around the table, George was short and round. He wore rather thick glasses, and dressed exclusively in dark grey. He had been a banker when he was alive.

"Phooey, no," said Martin. "Moselle is too sweet for my tastes. This is a white Bordeaux."

"Ah yes, you and your trips to Europe," remarked Albert, the third man. Albert's head came very nearly to a point on top; his whole face was dominated by a thick bushy light brown mustache that made his forehead appear even smaller by comparison. Albert was the thinnest of the three, and the youngest, in his early sixties. His face bore an expression somewhat like a pirate's; you could almost expect him to pull out a sword at any moment—but with a smile behind his eyes.

Martin picked up the bottle and looked at the label. "I used to pick this up earlier, when I lived in New York. Wonderful city, New York. You can find nearly all of Europe there."

Albert leaned back and stretched. "Ahhh. New York, Europe, California. Martin, I don't know how you did it on your salary. That is to say, I know now, but I'm amazed at the patience it took to save all the time. With me, money came in one hand and went out the other. George ought to have been the one to travel, he's the only one of the three of us who never had to relearn an occupation."

Remembrance of Meals Past

Martin raised his eyebrows and toasted Albert with his glass. "You can also travel if you have married wealth."

Albert threw his head back and guffawed. "Erika was too heavy for that. Anyway, she liked her farm too much. Can't leave cows and pigs for more than a day at a time."

George Benson shook his head. "Erika was a good woman. I was like her in many ways, we both liked peace and quiet. I had to go to New York for a conference once. Too large. Too busy. I was a nervous wreck after two days, and it took me a week to recover. Everyone shouted, and they were all in a hurry. That's why I liked Seattle, a small town then, not much bigger than Riga was."

Albert snorted. "From lawyer and judge to insurance clerk." He stared at Martin, who sat perfectly straight in his chair, and with his imagination dressed him in the black robes of the time he'd known Martin in Latvia. "There. That's the way you ought to look. Proud, as you were before the Russians invaded. Hmm." He nodded his head at the look he created.

Martin closed his eyes and shook his shoulders, shrugging off the voluminous cloth, waving his arms until it disappeared completely. "No, no. a thousand times no." After a moment he opened his eyes, affirmed the blue wool V-neck sweater, and relaxed. "That was the past. Even Seattle is the past, but here in this apartment my daughter and I used to enjoy good times. This is why I chose to come back and visit, it is what I wish to remember, and you, my old friends, also."

Albert took his wine glass and stood up from the small table. You couldn't truly call it a dining room, since the apartment consisted of one large room. A curtain divided the bedroom from the living-dining half; a counter further separated the kitchen from the living space. "The room of an ascetic and an idealist. Yes, Martin, this looks like the way you would have had it." He walked around the room and stood at the corner window. "This seems to be a busy street. Did the noise bother you?" A distant horn honked, and the building shook from a passing truck.

Martin shook his head. "No, as long as you don't open the window. But I seldom did. Anyway, it's ten stories above the street. The noise dissipates before it reaches this high." The sounds of traffic abated, and the surroundings became quiet once again.

George turned his chair to face the windows. The lights of the city sparkled around a dark curve, which was the water. "Such a view. The Space Needle, the bay. It must have been pleasant here. I would like to have visited you here."

Martin smiled. "You could have come at any time. I would have welcomed you."

"One never comes unless one is asked."

Albert returned to stand by the table. "No. That is not true. You can go anywhere you please, as long as you have a clear view of where you intend to go."

"Well, that's just it. I never knew where Martin lived, or I might have come sooner. But it's good to finally be together once again." He turned to Martin. "How long has it been?"

Martin pursed his lips, took a sip of wine. "Let's see. You left when I—no, after—I returned from California. That was when I just retired." He turned to Albert. "But you—you had to go first! My daughter grew up in the space we've been apart."

George sipped his wine, staring at nothing in particular. "Seems like only yesterday."

Martin looked at Albert. He leaned back in his chair, one arm on the table, one elbow hooked around the chair back. "I never forgave your wife after that accident. But she was Adele's friend, so I had to continue to be sociable."

Albert chuckled. "Funny. The women are all still together: Adele, Margaret, and Erika. I didn't think they had much in common other than being the wives of three old friends."

"They can have one another." Martin made a spitting motion.

"Oh, no," said George, "they're not still together. I saw Margaret not long ago, she's remarried A younger man this time, and they've moved to the suburbs. Quite a different crowd she moves in now, I'd say."

Albert laughed, stroking his mustache, his entire body shaking. "So you've turned into a peeping Tom now, eh? I would never have expected that from you. Quite an amusement, I agree."

George waved his hand at Albert, frowning. He leaned forward, his finger tracing the grain of the wood tabletop, the corners of his mouth turned down. "Margaret always was hot-blooded. She needed more excitement than I could give her. She sapped my strength. That's probably why I had a heart attack. That, and the job."

Martin reached to the counter behind him for a plate of crackers and pâté, placed it on the table. "I told you. Let's not mull over what's past. What's dead is dead. So to speak." The other two laughed, and Martin raised his glass once again. "Eat, drink and be merry, I've always said. Let's enjoy one another's company while we're still all together."

Albert clinked Martin's glass with his own. "To us."

"To us!"

"To us."

The three men tipped their heads back and emptied their glasses.

The short blonde woman pulled the bottle from the bottom shelf of the refrigerator. "Here, Brian. You open this."

"What? Wine, on a Tuesday?"

The woman laughed. "Chicken Kiev requires white wine." She reached into a cupboard, pulling out a tin of pâté and a box of crackers. "And this is the appetizer."

Brian frowned. "Such a fancy dinner in mid-week. Ann, you're not pregnant or something, are you? Here, let me see your temperature." He reached a hand to her forehead.

Ann pushed his hand away, laughing. "Silly! I just felt like it, that's all. I was thinking of wine and pâté all day today, I don't know why. I think I must have dreamed of it. Look, I got a white Bordeaux. The label looked so nice. The man at the store said it would go well with chicken, so I made chicken. With the help of the deli, I mean." She emptied the tin of pâté on the plate, surrounded it with crackers, put the plate on the countertop and walked around the half-wall into the small dining area. Her husband carried the bottle and two glasses, followed her to the small table and sat down. After pouring the wine, he raised his glass, propping his elbow on the table. "What shall we toast? We have to toast something."

Ann pushed her hair off her forehead, turned to stare out the window. "Let's see. We could toast the view. Or Mrs. Gredzens for not raising the rent." She turned back to face Brian. "Or we could just toast ourselves."

"To us," Brian said, extending his glass.

"To us," said Ann, clinking her glass against his. She took a sip and giggled.

"Get some up your nose?"

"No, I was just thinking. Why do we have that awful curtain there? It doesn't match anything we've got."

"We need something as a room divider. Mrs. Gredzens was good enough to let us use that one."

"Heaven knows who had it before us. It never used to bother me, but now I'm getting tired of looking at it. Can we get something else, Brian?"

"Look, Ann, curtains are expensive. There's no shop here. I can't build you a screen. Your sewing machine is still packed up in the basement, you haven't touched it in the three months we've been living here." He cut the chicken into small pieces, spreading them out over his plate. He put the knife and fork down without taking a bite.

"Tell you what. If we can afford it, let s buy ourselves a Christmas gift. A new room divider. Something that won't cut off our view of the Space Needle and Elliott Bay."

"Oh, Brian. That's a good idea." She raised her glass again. "To Christmas."

Brian laughed, wiped his mouth and raised his glass to hers. "To Christmas."

Martin wore a chef's apron and oven mitts on his hands. He carried a steaming plate from the oven to the small round table. "I'm sorry, I don't have a chef's hat. You'll have to tolerate my gray hair."

Remembrance of Meals Past

George squinted through his glasses at the bird on the plate. "That's too small for a turkey and too big for a chicken."

Albert laughed. "What's in your head? This is St. Martin's Day. Everyone knows you always serve goose on St. Martin's."

Martin removed the mitts from his hands, removed the apron and hung them all carefully on a hook. He picked up a bottle of red from the counter, poured a small quantity into his glass, swirled the red liquid, sniffed it, then sipped. He made chewing motions with his mouth and after a moment, swallowed "Ahh, perfect."

Albert raised a finger. "In death everything is perfect."

Martin frowned, shaking his head at Albert. "Don't spoil the mood." He poured the wine into everyone's glasses, then sat down. "George, you look puzzled."

George turned in his chair, looking behind him. "That curtain. It looks different. What did you do?"

Martin laughed. "What did *I* do? You mean, what did Mrs. Gredzens let those people who live here do." The curtain became filmy, nearly transparent, and through it, the three saw the rattan folding screen. Martin shrugged. "The husband picked it out. His taste is somewhat better than the women. I don't truly object to the screen, but it interferes. I have to concentrate harder." The yellow curtain faded in and out of sight, and finally became solid again. "There." Martin turned to the goose and began to carve it.

Albert attacked a piece as soon as it was served. "Excellent. You always were a good cook, Martin. But I remember it was always Adele who cooked, never you."

"She wouldn't let me. She hated goose, said it was too fat. She was probably right, but nevertheless I liked it. And the leg of lamb!" He slapped his forehead. "Ah, how she could massacre it!"

Albert drank from his glass. "Don't think too much about it, you might bring her here. I've done that before, you know." He looked at George, who was staring at the window. Standing at the window, looking out, was the somewhat transparent image of a short blonde woman wearing a long flannel nightgown. She did not move, she simply stood to stare. "One of us, or asleep?" Albert asked.

George crossed his hands in his lap. "She's pretty. Reminds me a little of my niece." He turned to Martin. "She lives here?"

Martin nodded, his mouth full of goose. "She travels in her dreams."

Albert smiled. "Yes, she is pretty. A sweet woman who means well." He turned to Martin. "Mrs. Gredzens will tell her about you."

"That doesn't bother me. Neither of those two women are developed enough to interfere with our nightly parties. She may believe she dreamed about us, but she'll never imagine it was anything but a fantasy."

George piled pieces of goose onto his fork. "But this one's very sympathetic. She's already sensitive to us. She might happen to notice us one of these nights, and then what would we do?"

Martin waved his knife and fork. "Tell her to go back to sleep. Such people are very receptive to suggestions. See? She's already gone."

Albert and George turned to the window again. The figure had returned to bed.

Brian looked at his wife over the newspaper. "Something wrong?"

Ann held the coffee cup between her hands, breathing in the steam. She shook her head.

Her husband folded the paper and dropped it on the floor. "Come on. You can tell me."

"You're not going to believe me. I'm not even sure what it is I want to say. Brian, I had a strange dream last night. I was standing at that window, looking out. I felt I was being watched. I turned around and saw three old men at the dining table. They were eating, having a party, laughing and talking. It was as if I was standing outside the window, looking in. It was their place, not ours. A strange feeling, like I didn't belong there."

"You do belong. *We* belong. It's just a dream, Ann."

"That's not the end of it. I met Mrs. Gredzens at the mailbox this morning, and asked her about the man who used to live here before us." She leaned forward, staring. "Brian, she showed me pictures. It's the same man in my dream."

"I thought I was the man of your dreams."

"Oh, stop that." She pushed her plate aside. "His name was Martin Andreika, he used to be a lawyer in the old country, Latvia. He used to travel a lot, and on one of his trips to Europe he fell down a flight of stairs, or something like that. The doctor put him in the hospital when he came back home. He died within a week."

Brian swirled the mashed potatoes and peas into a green and white pile on his plate. "So you've got a good imagination. Or a good memory. Mrs. Gredzens loves talking about the old days, and she's always inviting us down for cakes and cookies and showing us her photo albums. You've probably seen his picture before, and now you're dreaming about him." He snorted. "Now I get to be jealous of a dead man."

Ann shook her head slowly, looking down at her hands. "That's not good enough for me. I'm going to do something about it. There's a bookstore down the street that can put me in touch with people who can help me."

"You watch too many movies!" He threw his knife down; it bounced off the table and landed on the floor. "Don't go getting yourself into trouble. Those people who claim they're psychic only want your money. They can only mess up your head, and I like you the way you are."

Ann sighed and said nothing.

George looked at the label on the bottle. "Beaujolais. What's for dinner tonight?"

Martin carried a plate to the table. "Leg of lamb. It's springtime, the lamb is fresh and good. And I have to make larger meals, now that we have a guest." He winked at the young woman seated at the table.

"I just hope Brian doesn't roll over and poke me in the ribs, like he did last time. It's quite a shock to return to one's body that suddenly. Not to mention embarrassing." Ann turned to the corner and pointed. "That's a beautiful desk. Did it come from Latvia?"

"Phooey, no. You cannot carry the furniture through Germany during a war. I bought that at Ernst and finished it myself. My daughter has it now. I must congratulate you on your progress. You have achieved much in the last five months."

Ann smiled. "I didn't get very far with that medium. But when I started studying astral travel, that's when things took off. It helped to be able to practice every day when Brian was at work."

"Astral travel, phooey. You should study something serious." Martin went to the desk and pulled a book from under a pile of paper. "Here."

Ann looked at the title. "Palmistry?"

Martin nodded. "The lines of your hand. You are born with the future written on the palms of your hands." He shook his head. "My daughter insists on studying astrology. She didn't listen, either. There was a woman in Latvia who read palms She was very good, she foretold my entire life."

George took a sip of wine. "I thought you had more imagination than that. If she foretold your life, you would have the power to change it."

Martin shook his head. "No. No. There are things that are written, and they do not change. Some things do, but these are not written as lines on your hand."

Ann looked around the table and discovered that Albert was no longer there. "Where did he go?"

Martin tipped his head back and emptied his glass. "He has been fading in and out. Soon it will be his time."

"His time? What do you mean?"

"He is preparing for the next life. Soon he will be reborn." He hung his head. "I will miss him, he was my best friend. I lost him twenty years ago to a car accident, and now ..." Martin's voice faded.

"There's still so much I have to learn." Ann pushed the pieces of lamb around on her plate. "Can't he still come to visit? I mean, look at me, I'm still alive, and yet I'm here visiting with you."

Martin shook his head and took another sip of wine. "You had the dedication to follow the rigorous training that was necessary. You also are blessed with a natural psychic instinct, which did not hurt. But when a soul is reborn into a new body, all prior memories are locked up, made inaccessible. At death, the memories of the past, as well as some knowledge of the future, are released, but upon birth, we become blind again. He will no longer be Albert, bur someone else. He will not come back."

George laughed quietly, his shoulders shaking. "You are right, Martin. I cannot understand now how stupid I used to be about my wife. Now it all seems so clear to me."

Ann leaned back in her chair, stretching her arms. "In a way, I almost envy you. Here you are, enjoying yourselves continually, doing what you want, seeing and knowing everything. Why would Albert want to go back to a more limited existence?"

"No, dear lady, the existence is not more limited. In part, these parties seem effortless because we do not have the physical needs and instincts to distract our minds. For a while, we get together and act out the fantasies we never were able to achieve during our lifetimes. Take me, for instance. I rarely was allowed to cook in my household, and by the time I divorced, all of my old friends were dead and gone. What could I do but dream about the old country and how it used to be? And now that I am free, so to speak. I can satisfy all my old needs. But still, they do not satisfy, because I know this is all created by our mutual imaginations. We are all creatures of the earth; we are not satisfied until we experience the physical manifestations of our desires. You see the same things now that we do because you have trained yourself to see more clearly. Others might pass by and sense our gaiety, but awake with other dreams or perhaps none at all. And eventually, the astral body itself passes away. Soon, George and I will no longer desire these gatherings. Then you will have your apartment to yourself."

"Oh, no," cried Ann. "Just when I was getting good at this, you're going to disappear on me."

Martin wiped his mouth with a napkin. "You must not hold us back. It will cause grief both to you and to us. Spend your time with the living, not with the dead."

Ann hung her head, a weak smile on her lips. "I'm still surprised at how this turned out. I expected more drama, I guess. Brian was right, I've seen too many movies."

George lifted his glass. "It's not for nothing that they say 'from dust we come.' Dust is not very romantic, but mountains are made from a great pile of it. You must remember that this present life will become, after death, another one of your past lives. How banal, *n'est-ce past?*"

Ann laughed and lifted her glass in salute. "To banality."

Brian carved into the leg of lamb, and a slice fell away. "Hey, Ann. this isn't done. You trying to poison us?"

"Brian, it's only just barely pink inside. That's the way it ought to be, there's more flavor that way."

"I wish I knew where you get all these ideas. Goose and sauerkraut, duck with orange sauce, lamb that screams when you slice it." He turned to the other couple seated at the table. "She won't tell me who's teaching her to cook like this."

Ann's eyes twinkled. "I told you, its subliminal. I learn in my sleep. You'd be amazed at what you miss by not dreaming, Brian." She turned to the other woman at the table. "So when is the baby due?"

"In about 10 weeks. We've decided that if it's a boy, we're going to name him Albert. If it's a girl, I don't know yet."

Culinary Divorce or, the Souring of a Relationship

I IGNORED ALL THE WARNING SIGNS: my astrologer friend, who said Pisces natives exercise control by being passive/aggressive; the nightmares that occurred every night for the entire week before I took the plunge; my cat. who sensed impending doom and ran away one week before the wedding, never to be seen again. But I married Rick anyway.

Before the marriage, I used to pride myself on being a good cook. My grandmother, who was part French, learned culinary arts in Paris, and I had a cousin who was a professional chef. My father also prepared his own specialty dishes, including a leg of lamb to kill for. Meatloaf was one of the first things my mother taught me to cook, and I felt rejected when I realized my new husband didn't appreciate most of the things I loved to cook.

Rick's mother Nancy walked around her hardwood-floored house wearing high-heeled hard plastic "slippers." To me, the word home (not to mention slippers) is synonymous with comfort, and I can't imagine being comfortable in high-heeled plastic shoes. She didn't own a hairbrush or comb, went to the beauty salon once a week to have her hair washed and styled, and slept with her head wrapped in toilet paper.

One Christmas she bestowed upon me a gift of a pair of high-heeled plastic slippers very much like the ones she wore. They were so uncomfortable that I quietly gave them away to Goodwill. Nancy couldn't speak a sentence without mangling at least two words or massacring a cliché ("the foot's on the wrong shoe" was her favorite). But she knew the Latin name of every plant that grew in our area, including the weeds. She and her husband had been married since they were both nineteen and now, more than thirty years later, she raged with jealousy every time another woman came near her beloved Jake.

I suppose, in retrospect, the universe was giving me an opportunity to develop assertiveness. But, if Nancy was the image of a self-assured, assertive woman, I didn't want to have anything to do with it. I'm sure I could have come up with a better model. Unfortunately, Nancy was Rick's model for the perfect wife, and ultimately I found I didn't match up, in his eyes.

Recently, my doctor suggested that I need to eat more fermented foods. She mentioned the usual: yogurt, kefir, and sauerkraut. At the mention of sauerkraut, I was startled to realize I hadn't eaten it in a long time.

Sauerkraut is part of my Latvian heritage. Latvia, like Russia, is located far to the north. Because of its location and climate, typically only winter vegetables thrive there. That's why Russians and Latvians have so many cabbage dishes—because cabbage is one of the few crops you can count on to thrive there.

Latvian sauerkraut is very much like Alsatian sauerkraut. It can be either baked in the oven or cooked over slow heat on the stove. Many women add either apples or potatoes, some add fresh cabbage to the already soured kraut. Most recipes specify adding sugar, which helps it brown when baked in the oven. Universally, though, the main spice to add is caraway seeds. It's served with either pork chops or sausages, and typically you're supposed to add plenty of "good, healthy" fat. (And by that they don't mean canola oil!) I think my mother used bacon grease, which she always stored in an empty can that she kept on the counter.

When I married my now-ex-husband, I didn't realize how finicky he was about food. Tomatoes and cucumbers were forbidden; I could fix myself a salad with them I chose to, but I would probably

Remembrance of Meals Past

have been banished from the house entirely if I tried to give any to him.

I already knew about his tomato fetish. He refused to eat tomatoes in any form except spaghetti sauce; he abhorred the texture. What I didn't realize was that every time I brought a tomato into the house, he would produce a string of expletives and pretend to vomit. Not just once, not randomly, but every time. Every time. Even when I assured him they were for me only, as a salad to bring with me to work.

If it had been just tomatoes, I might have been able to ignore it. But in addition to what the French termed "apple of love," Rick's list of forbidden foods included cucumbers, radishes, onions, and meatloaf: everything I had previously survived on. On the positive side, I learned to make a huge variety of salads that didn't contain foods he refused to eat.

Included in the long list of foods he refused to eat was sauerkraut. I suspected his only experience of it was a heap of it, cold, plain, plopped onto a plate directly from the jar. No wonder he didn't like it. I kept trying to convince him how different it tasted.

"Take just a tiny bite," I'd say. But no. He refused.

I had to invite friends over for dinner to be able to serve sauerkraut. When I did that once, our friends remarked to Rick, "It's really delicious. You should try some, Rick." But he adamantly refused, even at the prodding of his best friend.

It was during a vacation in Europe that things turned around.

Rick was always the kind of person who, on the subject of travel, said: "See America first!" But I, with my background in French language and literature, hadn't been to France in many years, and I was dying to go. So, one year, Rick agreed to a vacation in France.

We stayed in Paris, of course, visiting museums and shops and restaurants. Rick marveled at the art in the Louvre, the cathedrals, especially Notre Dame. We spent a lot of time walking. I introduced him to the English bookstore on the Seine, Shakespeare, and Company. He reveled in chocolate croissants for breakfast and loved the coffee.

Not far from our hotel was an Alsatian restaurant; we tried it out one evening. When I saw sauerkraut on the menu, I ordered it.

When it came, to my utter shock and dismay, Rick asked me if he could try a bite.

"Of course," I replied, pushing the plate nearer to him. He took a bite, chewing slowly, savoring the taste. He then nodded, pushing the plate back to me. "If you can make it taste like that, then I will let you make sauerkraut for dinner."

I was so mad I didn't know what to say. I didn't want to make a scene in a public restaurant, especially in Paris, so I fumed internally and kept my mouth shut. How did he know that I *couldn't* make it taste like that? He'd never tasted my sauerkraut before, so how could he make any judgment at all?! What right did he have to "allow" me to cook what I wanted to eat?

After we returned home from the vacation, I was pleasantly surprised that Rick actually had liked France. He hadn't had to worry about communicating, since most of the time I was the one speaking, and I speak French very well.

I later realized—and my friends agreed—that I'd been too soft, too accommodating. I should have been more like his mother and put my foot down. I suppose, in that respect, I was as passive/aggressive as Rick himself was.

Ultimately, our differences strained the relationship too far, and we separated, then divorced. The difference in food tastes was only one of the symptoms.

But now I can eat tomatoes, cucumbers, and sauerkraut to my heart's content, without having to worry about someone lurking over my shoulder saying. "Yuck! I'm not eating that!"

Comfort Foods and Cravings

When I was little, my parents and I would go to Pike Place Market every Saturday to do the shopping for the week. In those days, there were two lanes for cars: one for cars that were passing right through, another for cars that were stopped, waiting. Dad would sit in our 1954 Chevrolet in the waiting lane, while my mother and I strolled around to shop. If my father was lucky enough to find a parking spot, he'd join us. When they bought the car, they'd asked me what I wanted to name it.

"Veronica," I immediately replied. I loved that name.

"No," they said. "That name is too long. We'll call it Laura." (I now understand that Veronica was too foreign a name for them, and one they probably couldn't remember or pronounce.)

One of my mother's regular stopping points was Milwaukee Foods, which sold mostly sausages and lunch meats. My mother would order something—I can't remember exactly what, probably some bologna (pronounced like the city in Italy, *not* pronounced "baloney")—which would accompany us in sandwiches for lunch. I, being shorter than the counter, would stare at the array of wieners and thick sausages that were the staple of eastern European cultures such as ours. My mother and the woman behind the counter would speak German with one another. Invariably, as my mother was paying for her purchases, the woman behind the counter would hand me a nice, fresh wiener to munch on. I would look up at her and smile; she was round, a bit rounder than my mother, always smiling, and had dark chestnut hair the same color as my mother's. I could tell there was genuine affection in her eyes. "Say thank you," my mother reminded me. I thanked the lady behind the counter and savored the free gift.

Fast-forward about thirty years. I've taken up competitive crew—rowing—like my favorite recreation. It's demanding, exhausting at times, but immensely satisfying for me. It provides companionship and an opportunity not only co exercise outdoors, but on the water, which I love. It also provides an opportunity to travel, if we choose to participate in regional or national regattas.

That year, the regional championships were held in Vancouver, Washington, about a three-hour drive from Seattle. Crew members carpooled, we spent a weekend sharing hotel rooms, eating together, growing together, getting too much sunshine, and in general having a rousing good time. That time, I carpooled with a woman I'll call Anne.

I wasn't particularly fond of Anne. She and I had participated the previous year in the San Diego Crew Classic. We had high hopes of winning but came in second by a few hairs. The rest of us shrugged our shoulders, talked about what we could have done better, then celebrated our second-place medal and went out to enjoy San Diego, dinner at a good restaurant, and walks along the beach before our flight home. Anne spent the entire time after the race, as well as several days and weeks afterwards, mumbling, agonizing, and questioning where we went wrong. We all told her to get over it, but she persisted in her wailing and gnashing of teeth. No one wanted to be with her. I had to sit next to her on the three-hour plane trip back to Seattle, listening to her complaints and whines.

Anne and her husband were devoutly religious; he worked to support her, so she didn't have to have a day job like most of the rest of us. She had the financial security to buy her own single shell, and the leisure time to paddle around in it during the day. I always associated her with the 1950s and the lifestyle portrayed in the TV series "Ozzie and Harriet," or "Leave It to Beaver." Even though Anne was less than five years older than me, I felt an entire generation gap between us.

Remembrance of Meals Past

Even more significant was the cultural gap: Anne, born in the U.S. of American parents, was American through and through. I was born in a refugee camp in Germany of immigrant parents, and have carried through my life the memory of hardships both physical as well as emotional.

I will never forget the day my mother came home from work crying. She worked in the accounting office of a large department store and had to answer the phone at lunchtime when everyone else was away. As it often happens, my mother's English was better and less flawed than my father's, even though he'd been speaking the language longer. I hadn't met anyone who couldn't understand my mother's speech. That day, she'd answered the phone at lunchtime, and an irate customer had been on the other end. After a very brief conversation during which she told him everyone was out and there was no one there to help him, he'd replied, "Give me someone who speaks English!"

At Christmas, Anne's family and mine sing different songs.

I carpooled with Anne at that time because it was my last choice aside from driving by myself in a fifteen-year-old car. The friends I wanted to share a ride with already had a full car; others were leaving at a time that was not convenient for me. Even though Anne's company wasn't ideal for me, I knew that at least we could be pleasant with one another. I don't recall the trip down to Vancouver very well, but the trip back was remarkable because of the stop we made along the way.

Rowers are always eating because rowing takes so much out of you. You can't eat before a race because the violent exercise interferes with digestion, and also because a heavy stomach interferes with a good row. We'd spent hours putting boats back on the trailer after the races, then gathering up our belongings. It had been a long time since we'd eaten, and Anne and I were both hungry. We stopped along the way at a small restaurant that promised home-cooked food. It sounded good to Anne, and also to me. We sat down at a table and opened up a menu.

"Oh," exclaimed Anne. "Macaroni and cheese! I'll have that. Comfort food, that's what I need." She hugged herself, and told me of the times she'd come home from school and her mother would fix macaroni and cheese in a warm, sunny kitchen.

Words, all just words. Macaroni was a dish that wasn't in my mother's repertoire, and when you say "cheese" to me, I think of Stilton, Brie, or Camembert. Cheddar is as foreign to me as tofu is to others. I wanted good old-fashioned sausage with sauerkraut. That smacked of home-cooking to me. When I thought of sauerkraut, my body conjured up images of holiday tables groaning with wealth, surrounded by friends and family, and a steaming hot dish full of sweet, brown sauerkraut full of onions and apples, covered by pork chops and sausages, swimming in fat. Yum!

"I want some sauerkraut," I said.

Anne wrinkled up her nose and made disgusted noises. She couldn't relate to sauerkraut: "it's so—well—sour!" She giggled at her pun.

I shook my head. "No, it isn't, not if you fix it right." And I told her how my mother and her friends would cook it. She agreed, that with those ingredients it probably wouldn't be so sour. But it was obvious that her feelings toward sauerkraut were the same as my feelings toward macaroni and cheese casseroles.

The menu was indeed full of home-cooked classics such as meatloaf; tuna melt; macaroni and cheese; turkey with mashed potatoes, gravy and cranberries, and various kinds of salads and sandwiches. Up until that time, I'd considered myself American, but when I looked at the menu, nothing sounded like good home cooking to me. The closest thing to what I wanted was a Reuben sandwich, so I ordered it. Rye bread and sauerkraut were two classics I'd grown up with.

I should have had the meatloaf—meatloaf is pretty standard, no matter what part of the world you're in. The spices are different, and some cultures use lamb with pine nuts instead of beef with onions and Worcestershire. But somehow, to me, they're all very similar, and equally comforting. Maybe it's the texture.

Remembrance of Meals Past

The rye bread was almost white, with one or two caraway seeds sprinkled through. The rye bread I'd grown up with was dark brown, loaded with caraway seeds, and solid enough to give you a good chew. This bread dissolved in your mouth in no time at all. It was like the white bread I begged my mother for when I was little so that I could compress an entire slice into a ball the size of a pea and pop in my mouth. The Reuben sandwich was OK, but not home cooking. Not my home, at least.

The corned beef was good, just the right spices and very satisfying. Meat is always satisfying to me, especially sausage, and I'm sure it's because of the lady at the Milwaukee Foods stand, who always had a wiener and a special smile for me. I hope she's happy, wherever she is.

But the sauerkraut was American. Barely lukewarm, and most definitely sour. Even I didn't like it, and I love sauerkraut. I ate the Reuben sandwich sadly, remembering.

If my parents had settled in Ohio rather than Washington State, I might not have had the same problem. I visited a friend after she'd moved to Cleveland, and when we walked around her neighborhood, I was amazed to see how many ethnic restaurants there were in a small space: two German, one Lithuanian, several Russian restaurants. Over there, I could have found all the sauerkraut I wanted, and it would have been just like home-cooked. But in Seattle—Lithuanian? How do you spell that? There's a restaurant at the north end of Lake Washington that offers wiener schnitzel, so it's called German, the only German restaurant in ninety miles. Don't even ask about Russian restaurants, there aren't any (or weren't, then).

In the years that followed, Anne and I often carpooled to distant regattas. Sometimes others joined us. It was usually a polite ride, with polite conversation, but I never felt Anne was a woman I could open the inside of my heart to. We were just too different.

Anne was very competitive, too, in more than just crew racing. While sitting behind her one day, I noticed she had white roots growing underneath her brown-black hair. She boasted that she was going through menopause with no problems and no hormones, but in a hotel bathroom one regatta weekend, I discovered a bottle of Premarin with her name on it. And if the boat she was in didn't take first place, she was sick and miserable for days, and never let anyone else forget about the loss.

Anne was absent from crew for an entire season. I later heard that she'd developed breast cancer. Some psychologists and New Age philosophers say that cancer results from an excess of anxiety combined with repressed emotions, or not letting go of the past, or an inability to adapt to change. The part of me that didn't like Anne was whispering "See? Her lying ways and obsession with not losing finally got to her!" But another part of me, the part which enjoys warm fires, happy homes, and matronly women offering me sausages, hugs, and kisses, refused to be so cold. I felt guilty for not liking her.

Members of our crew ran together as a group in the Race for the Cure. On the same weekend, more crew members drove down to Portland to participate in the Row for the Cure, dedicating their trip to Anne. I had other plans that weekend and could not participate in either. I marveled that the same women who had avoided Anne in San Diego after our second-place ribbon were now the ones who were cheering her on. I wondered if karma hadn't thrown us together because I, like Anne, held on to grudges and failures, refusing to adapt to changing times. They say that the people you dislike the most are the ones who resemble you.

After some time, Anne started showing up at our crew social events sporting a big grin, although she hadn't returned to practice. Someone started planning a party to celebrate Anne's victory over the big "C". Three women put together a quilt made of rowing t-shirts to give Anne as a gift (we all had several dresser drawers' worth of regatta shirts, a lifetime supply for us as well as our extended families and the entire neighborhood). The party was to be a potluck, everyone bringing a favorite dish to fit the theme "comfort food."

Remembrance of Meals Past

Susan, a woman who usually sits behind me in boats, asked me what I was planning to bring to the potluck. "You always bring such exotic dishes, I'll bet this one'll be special."

I thought for a brief moment. True, I always enjoyed bringing Latvian specialties that displayed my ancestral heritage and pride. I loved to bring sauerkraut, or a good loaf of rye bread, or delicate Latvian pastries. But not this time. "I'm just bringing macaroni and cheese," I replied.

"Oh, that's right," Susan said, nodding. "Comfort food."

Meatloaf Afternoon

My guardian angel has a wicked sense of humor. I know all this happened because of the meditation I did that morning. Whenever I take up a task with the purpose of cleansing and purifying, it always works better than I hope it will.

One of my husband Harry's strong points was his domestic skills. We both loved to cook; whenever he was too tired to cook, I fixed the meals; whenever I was too tired to cook, he took over. He even cleaned well: he did a far better job on the kitchen and bathroom than I ever did, and even willingly did the laundry. This is any woman's idea of a perfect husband, I kept telling myself. He even brought me flowers, for no special reason. I have since learned that this is the mark of a man who has severely traditional views on the relationship between men and women, one who likes to manipulate his spouse into feeling guilty and dutiful. However, this sunny August day also preceded the counseling sessions a few years later, so I was not appropriately armed with this knowledge at the time.

Whenever I'm faced with a situation in which I'm not getting what I want, I always ask myself what I did wrong. Having studied astrology, Tarot, and the occult sciences as well as having dabbled in Buddhism, I knew about illusion, *Maya*, how we deceive ourselves. (Not to mention the Capricorn in me knows I'm responsible for everything that happens in the world.) A little bit of mindless living goes a long way; I, however, desired mindfulness, which might lead me to clarity and understanding. So, that morning, I retired to the back bedroom for a half hour and meditated. I practiced cleansing breathing, I focused on eliminating from my life that which did not belong. I resolved to purge myself of habit patterns and ways of thinking which were no longer true to my path in life. Whatever that was. I visualized clear light entering me and enlightening me, replacing the garbage I'd thrown out.

To provide a foundation for the meditation in real life, I decided to do some housecleaning, to get rid of clutter, throw out or give away objects I no longer needed. Harry was outdoors, building a fence in the back yard to prepare for the dog he wanted to get. "We've decided to get a Boxer," he declared to friends, one evening at a restaurant. I nearly dropped my fork. When did "we" decide to do this, I wondered. The only conversation I could recall was a single question he once asked: "how would you feel about owning a dog?"

Assuming it had been a theoretical question, I shrugged. "That depends," I said. "I don't want to be the one who winds up feeding it, walking it, taking care of it. You're gone a lot, you work long hours. Will you still have the energy to take it for walks?" (Later, in couples counseling, that question of mine somehow became my declared desire to be the one to walk the dog.)

How did I feel about purebreds, he asked. I told him there were thousands of dogs at the pound, free and waiting for an owner to love them. I also told him I'd always fantasized about owning a German Shepherd. "Harrumph," he grunted. "You never know what you're getting at the pound. Besides, everybody has a German Shepherd."

I am a thrifty person. Some would call me stingy. On Sundays, I plan and prepare the meals I will bring to work the following week. My mother taught me the value of cooking: why spend so much money on restaurant food when (1) you can fix it yourself for far less, (2) it you fix it yourself, you know exactly what's in it, and (3) it all comes out the other end, anyway. Today being Sunday, among my other chores, I thought about what I wanted to eat the following week.

Planning meals for myself has always been more satisfying than planning meals for Harry and myself, mainly because there's only one person to negotiate with, and I already agree with everything she likes and dislikes. I love meatloaf. It's the first thing my mother taught me to cook, and I do it well. It's a kind of comfort food for me. Harry hates it. To him, it's a symbol of poverty, and shows a lack of imagination. How often do you see meatloaf on the menus of famous restaurants, he would ask me. When I polled myself that day, I decided I wanted to pamper myself and fix meatloaf, to take with me for lunches the rest of the week. So, off to the grocery store, where I bought the necessary supplies.

Preparing the meatloaf was no big deal, I'd done it countless times before, and I stuck to the same recipe I'd always used, the one my mother taught me. But—the shock of all shocks—as the meatloaf was cooking in the oven, Harry came into the kitchen and asked me. "Is it OK if we have the meatloaf for dinner? I'd like to try it, the way you make it."

Wow. Would it be possible for me to win a competition with his mother? I told him yes, let's have it for dinner. Maybe I could convert Harry, one dish at a time, from his violent food likes and dislikes.

At that time, it was only midafternoon, sometime between two and three o'clock. A hot August afternoon. When it was done, I left the meatloaf on the counter to cool. Around five, we ate the meatloaf for dinner. Harry approved. What a success for me, I thought. I refrigerated the leftovers to take with me for lunches the following week.

When I woke the next morning, I didn't feel at my best but went to work anyway.

By 10 a.m., it was obvious I couldn't stay at work all day, I was feeling too bad. I went home. When I got home, I discovered Harry was already there, in the bathroom, with diarrhea. Imagine two people with severe diarrhea sharing one bathroom.

After a trip to the doctor's office, we realized we had food poisoning. The meatloaf was the obvious culprit. My big mistake was leaving it on the counter for two or three hours at room temperature to cool. This had never happened to me before, and when I came back home, I sadly threw out the remaining meatloaf. Never waste food, my mother taught me. It seemed like a colossal waste, but what can you do when the food has become poison?

After that experience, Harry never asked for meatloaf again. Even though he liked it—even though I could have made it correctly—he never wanted to eat meatloaf again.

It took me a long time to try again. I did, with better results. But I can't ever cook meatloaf without remembering the "cleansing and purifying" experience. Meatloaf will remain my dish, not Harry's.

The Sins of the Fathers

THE SKIES ARE PERENNIALLY DARK AROUND you; the landscape is bleak. On the horizon flash occasional bursts of red and orange, followed by booming echoes and earth tremors. Bombs. You fear airplanes now; you no longer gaze at them in awe or wonder as you did in Latvia. Your father taught you caution; a woman alone is vulnerable, in need of protection, especially so now. Be suspicious, treat all persons you meet with distant respect until you are certain—are you ever?—they are allies and not traitorous German spies. Watch your words carefully so that they will not twist into a noose for your neck.

You are on your way to Dresden, but on the way there, you meet a woman you used to know in Latvia. "Do not go to Dresden," she says, "there is nothing there. Come with us, we are heading south and west." You take her advice. If nothing else, the companionship is welcome. Later, after hearing about the bombing of Dresden and how you miraculously avoided being killed, you begin to believe in fate moving through your life. Maybe there is hope after all.

Everyone you meet speaks of America. Escape to freedom is the desire in the hearts of millions. The agony of the Displaced person camp is only the first step toward this goal. Bunk beds and mattresses on the floor, rooms shared with other families, are simply stations of the cross, burdens to bear, prices to pay for future liberty. But here, at least, you are with fellow countrymen, most from Latvia. It is almost—but not quite—like being home again. And you are with family again, your two cousins and their husbands.

Remembrance of Meals Past

And when in this confused mass of humanity you recognize another face, you cry with relief, everything else becomes landscape, background for this face. See? A judge, who used to have a high position in society, once the most eligible bachelor in Latvia, now reduced to the same position as you. He has lost his robes and his superior smile; you have been stripped of your cozy life as the wife (now widow) of a captain in the Latvian army. No matter what your friends all call him stuck-up, egotistical, a lady-killer. You remember how filthy his apartment was when you visited him with your cousin Alise, his brother's wife. The dirty kitchen upset you so, you had to wash it. Alise scolded you, but Albert laughed and laughed.

The only remaining evidence of your social status is the sterling silver service, which weighs down your luggage and which has been buying provisions on the black market so you can survive. The knives now number two. All but one of the soup spoons is gone. The original twelve teaspoons and six forks remain, and—with any luck at all—can begin the hope chest for the daughter you hope to have when you reach the promised land. The precious jewelry—rubies, emeralds, and diamonds—never weighed much but were the first to go. It might have been nice to keep them in the family, but they were mostly your mother's earrings, and since you never pierced your ears, you don't have any use for them. You did keep the rubies because they were your birthstone; for some silly reason, you never told anyone you had them with you and kept them in a hidden pocket sewn in your dress. Tell your daughter, if you are ever lucky enough to have one, that it's a primitive ritual to pierce the ears, not something done by intelligent women in polite society. Buy something better in the new country after you get there.

It is Albert, the judge, who makes the suggestion first. That is as it should be; the man is the one to take charge. "I'm going to America," he says. "Are you also?"

If you conceive a child and go with him to the new homeland, then perhaps he will settle down in a family. He is attractive, no matter what the others used to say. "Callous, selfish, egotistical," they said. "He never returns social favors, he only accepts them," was the standing joke.

He takes you to the great hall of the DP camp, where the piano sits. Neither of you can play anything by memory, but there is also an old record player with a small collection of scratchy records. One night he plays arias from "Aida" for you, singing along in his marvelous rich voice. You go for a walk in the moonlight, unescorted, into the hills that surround the camp.

Sometime later you discover you are carrying a child. "Let's call her Aida," he suggests, in honor of their special evening.

"Don't be silly," you reply. "I am going to call her Mara. I have already decided."

Sudden doubt flashes through your mind. "What if it's a boy?"

Albert's eyes twinkle, his lips purse in amusement, his shoulders shake in silent laughter. "Well, throw it out the window if you don't want it."

You won't find out until many years later that there is another daughter, by the name of Carmen, honoring a similar occasion. You'll feel an instant bond of sympathy with her mother, who'll send Albert a bible for Christmas one year.

Thursday, April 24, 1986, the day the Duchess of Windsor died. A day to live in the memory of love affairs. It was a small restaurant, with a casual atmosphere, almost like a pub. The sun shone in the window, a sunny spring day. It was noon, and the small tables were rapidly filling up. A couple entered the restaurant: a tall man in a raincoat, accompanied by a blonde woman about six inches shorter. She watched heads turn; her companion was strikingly handsome, with neatly combed dark hair and a well-trimmed beard and mustache. Her stomach fluttered whenever she looked at him.

Something about him reminded her of her father; this puzzled her, because her father had been blond, and always clean-shaven. The young man wore the look of a businessman on his way up. He had the manner of a man who felt at ease in high-class restaurants. Having once been a waiter himself, on the receiving side of orders, Steve now masterfully gave them. It was Mara's first lunch date

Remembrance of Meals Past

with him; she hoped it would not be the last. This one, of all her men friends, might have met with her father's approval. Too bad he was no longer in touch; she was curious what he would have thought about Steve.

They took a table in a corner, behind a partition, near the bar. Steve asked the waitress what beers were on tap. She recited a long list. "I'll have a Guinness," he said. Mara nodded. "The same for me." She smiled, thinking what a happy coincidence he'd picked the same beer she'd already decided on.

Later, Mara could not remember how the conversation began, just that Steve led it. He asked her about herself, her life, her beliefs. She spoke of her background, about Latvia itself and the amber jewelry is produced. She added (she wasn't completely certain why) that she thought ear piercing was a barbarous practice. She spoke of immigrants, of how she felt about them coming to America and criticizing the very society they had fled to for freedom. True, these were her mother's words and her mother's thoughts, but Mara also believed them nevertheless. Mara heard her words echo off the walls and realized she was letting herself get carried away.

They spoke of Europe, and trips to Europe each were planning. When the waitress returned, Mara ordered a shepherd's pie; she'd always been curious about that dish, which she'd never had. Surprisingly, he requested the same. The waitress asked if they wanted another beer. Mara said no. Steve replied that he wanted to, but wouldn't be able to work if he did. The waitress smiled. "You'll just have to come back, then." Mara saw that her companion had made another conquest. *How easy it is for him to charm women*, she thought. Being his companion made her feel like a queen on a throne. But could she continue to attract his attention and his favor?

Out of the clear blue sky, he proclaimed, "I'm not the marrying kind." In spite of the words, she took it as a sign, along with the fact they had both ordered the same things, that something big was in the offing. He mentioned marriage, he must be thinking about it. She remembered her mother's stories about going to her father's apartment as washing the dirt and filch from his kitchen while he watched and laughed. She wondered what Steve's kitchen looked like, and if she would have the opportunity to see for herself. She would never again eat shepherd's pie without remembering this day.

"Do you like opera?" she asked, and when he replied yes, she added, "Aida is one of my favorites." She didn't tell Steve why.

Recipes

Cheesecake

For the cake:
3 8-ounce packages cream cheese
4 egg whites
1 cup of sugar
1 Tbsp vanilla

For the crust:
softened butter
bread or cracker crumbs

For the topping (added the last 5 min of baking):
2 cups (one pint) sour cream
2 Tbsp sugar
1/2 tsp vanilla

Preheat the oven to 350°. Smear an 8-inch springform pan with the softened butter. Dust with bread or cracker crumbs. Beat egg whites until stiff, blend in sugar.

In a separate bowl beat the cream cheese, sugar and vanilla until well mixed. Fold the egg whites into the cream cheese mixture and pour into the springform pan. Bake at 350° for 23 mm,

Remove the cake and turn the oven up to 475°. Gently spread the topping on the cake and bake an additional 5 minutes. Remove from the oven.

Chill for at least two hours.

Paella

The following is a recipe from the public domain, a relatively simple version.

6 Tbsp olive oil, divided
1 Tbsp paprika
2 tsp dried oregano
salt and pepper to taste
2 pounds skinless, boneless chicken breasts, cut into 2-inch pieces
3 cloves garlic, crushed
1 tsp crushed red pepper flakes
2 cups uncooked white rice
pinch saffron threads
1 bay leaf
1/2 bunch flat-leaf parsley, chopped
1-quart chicken stock
2 lemons, zested
1 onion, chopped
1 red bell pepper, coarsely chopped
1 pound chorizo sausage, casings removed and crumbled
1 pound shrimp, peeled and deveined

In a medium bowl, mix 2 tablespoons olive oil, paprika, oregano, and salt and pepper. Stir in chicken pieces to coat. Cover, and refrigerate.

Heat 2 tablespoons olive oil in a large skillet or paella pan over medium heat. Stir in garlic, red pepper flakes, and rice. Cook, stirring, to coat the rice with oil, about 3 minutes. Stir in saffron threads, bay leaf, parsley, chicken stock, and lemon zest. Bring to a boil, cover, and reduce heat to medium-low. Simmer 20 minutes, or until rice is done.

Meanwhile, heat 2 tablespoons olive oil in a separate skillet over medium heat. Stir in marinated chicken and onion; cook 5 minutes. Stir in bell pepper and sausage; cook 5 minutes. Stir in shrimp; cook, turning the shrimp, until both sides are pink.

Spread rice mixture onto a serving tray. Top with meat and seafood mixture.

Pasta

The recipe used in this story is extremely simple. Ingredients are pasta, water, and butter.

Bring a large pot of lightly salted water to a boil. Cook pasta in boiling water for 8 to 10 minutes or until al dente; drain.

Toss with butter. Serve. Eat.

Sautéed Boletus

Ingredients

Boletus mushrooms, 1 pound or enough to teed the number of people you are serving.

1 onion, chopped
Minced garlic (optional)
Butter, at least 2 Tbsp.
Cream

Clean the mushrooms and chop coarsely. Put several tablespoons butter into a pan, and heat until melted. Add the mushrooms, onion, and garlic, if you are using it, sauté until they are soft about 5 minutes. In the end, stir in some cream, either half-and-half or whipping cream. Add salt and pepper to taste.

This makes a tasty side dish.

Dough for Latvian Sheet Bread

1½ cups milk
½ cup soft butter or shortening
½ cup of sugar
2 tsp salt
1 lemon rind, grated
2 cubes or envelopes yeast
½ cup of warm water
2 slightly beaten eggs
7 cups sifted white flour

Heat milk, but do not boil. Add butter, sugar, salt and lemon rind.

Allow cooling. Dissolve yeast and add with eggs and half of the flour to the cooled milk mixture. Beat well. Gradually add remaining flour. Pour dough out on board and knead lightly, making an effort not to add too much more flour. The less flour, the more lender the bread. When the dough is smooth, place into a greased bowl, form into a ball, cover with a damp cloth and allow to rise in warm place approximately 1½ hours. Knead lightly again and allow to rise another ½ hour. Knead again and divide it into 2 parts. Place into 2 greased pans that have a small lip. Spread the dough so that it goes up the lip. Allow rising slightly. Place topping on dough and bake.

Use this dough for Apple Sheet Bread and Latvian Cheesecake.

Apple Sheet Bread

1/2 recipe of dough
1/2 cup sugar
Beaten egg for smearing
1/2 tsp. cinnamon
6-8 apples

Some cooks prefer sour apples for this, such as Granny Smith. My mother preferred softer ones, such as Golden Delicious. Your choice.

Smear dough out onto pan with egg. Pare and thinly slice sour apples. Put apple slices closely together on the dough and sprinkle with sugar and cinnamon. Allow rising. Bake at 400° for 30 minutes. You can cover the apples with aluminum foil for the first 20 minutes to make them more tender.

Latvian Cheesecake

½ dough recipe
Topping:
1 pint (16 oz) dry curd cottage cheese
½ cup of sugar
2 egg yolks
3 Tbsp sour cream
Optional: a handful of golden raisins
Slivered almonds for topping

Beat cottage cheese with sugar and sour cream. Add egg yolks one at a time. Mix in raisins, if you are using them. Spread onto the risen dough. Sprinkle with slivered almonds.

Bake in a 350° oven for 25-30 minutes.

Cut while still warm.

Paskha (Russian Easter Dessert)

This recipe uses the traditional clay flowerpot as a container because the clay absorbs all excess moisture.

CAUTION: this recipe is not cooked, and contains egg yolks. You may use a substitute if you wish.

1 package (12 oz) pitted prunes
2 pounds dry curd cottage cheese
¼ pound butter or margarine softened
1 3-oz package cream cheese, softened
3 egg yolks
½ cup of sugar
1 tsp vanilla
½ cup sour cream
½ cup chopped toasted almonds

Finely snip enough prunes to make one cup. Reserve the remainder for garnish.

In a food processor or blender, mix the cottage cheese, softened butter, and cream cheese. Turn into a bowl. In a separate bowl, beat the egg yolks with sugar and vanilla until thick. Beat in the sour cream. Add the egg-cream mixture to the cheese mixture and combine well. Stir in the chopped prunes and almonds.

Line a clean, new flowerpot, about 6 inches tall and 6 inches across at the top, with cheesecloth. Fill the lined flowerpot with the cheese mixture, and pack down with a spoon or spatula. Wrap the top of the cheese mixture with the ends of the cheesecloth. Put a plate on top of the cheese mixture, and put a weight on top of that. Put the flowerpot on a rack in a pan so that it can drain and refrigerate overnight.

The next day, unmold the platter. Carefully peel off the cheesecloth. Sliver some of the reserved prunes and arrange them in rows along the sides of the Paskha. Put a whole prune on top, and a row along the base.

Leg of Lamb

1 leg of lamb, bone-in (about 6 to 7 1/2 pounds)
1/4 cup olive oil
8 cloves garlic, halved
3 tablespoons chopped fresh rosemary leaves
1 tablespoon salt
2 teaspoons coarsely ground black pepper

Preheat the oven to 400°.

Using your hands, rub the lamb all over with the olive oil. Make small slits evenly around the lamb, and insert the garlic halves into the slits. Pat the rosemary evenly all over the surface of the meat. Season the meat with the salt and pepper and place the lamb in a roasting pan. Place the lamb in the oven and roast for 30 minutes. Reduce the oven temperature to 350°F and continue to cook for about 1 hour longer for medium-rare, or until a meat thermometer inserted into the center of the roast registers about 145-150° F (be careful that the thermometer does not touch the bone.) Remove lamb from pan and allow to rest for 10 to 15 minutes before carving.

Latvian Sauerkraut

3 jars (32 oz each) sauerkraut, drained (reserve the liquid)
1 large head green cabbage, shredded
1/3 lb bacon, cut into 1-inch pieces
3 medium onions, chopped
1 Tbsp caraway seeds
10-12 peppercorns
3 bay leaves
2 Granny Smith or Braeburn apples, peeled and sliced
1 cup brown sugar

In large stainless steel pot, sauté bacon until somewhat rendered, but not crisp. Add chopped onions; cook until soft and transparent. Add cabbage, sauerkraut and remaining ingredients.

You may need to add water or a little of the reserved liquid to keep the cabbage from burning. You can also add a half-cup or so of white wine if you wish.

Bring to a low simmer; cook covered for several hours on the stovetop or in the oven. If you bake in the oven, bake it uncovered for 3-4 hours at 350°, stirring occasionally.

Remove the bay leaves before serving.

Meatloaf

1 pound ground beef
1-2 slices white bread
1 egg
¼ onion, chopped
Salt and pepper to taste

Soak bread in milk and let stand. Combine ingredients and mix thoroughly.

Add salt and pepper to taste. You could also add some milk or water to make the meatloaf juicier.

Bake at 350° for one hour. If you do not eat it right away, cover with foil or plastic wrap and refrigerate.

Shepherd's Pie

For the potatoes:
1 1/2 pounds russet potatoes
1/4 cup half-and-half
2 oz unsalted butter
3/4 tsp kosher salt
1/4 tsp freshly ground black pepper
1 egg yolk

For the meat filling:
2 Tbsp vegetable oil
1 cup chopped onion
2 carrots, peeled and diced small
2 cloves garlic, minced
1½ pounds ground lamb
1 tsp kosher salt
½ tsp freshly ground black pepper
2 Tbsp all-purpose flour
2 tsp tomato paste
1 cup chicken broth
1 tsp Worcestershire sauce
2 tsp freshly chopped rosemary leaves
1 tsp freshly chopped thyme leaves
1/2 cup fresh or frozen corn kernels
1/2 cup fresh or frozen peas

Peel the potatoes and cut into ½-inch dice. Place in a medium saucepan and cover with cold water. Set over high heat, cover and bring to a boil. Once they are boiling, uncover, decrease the heat to maintain a simmer and cook until tender, approximately 10 to 15 minutes. Place the half-and-half and butter into a microwave-safe container and heat in the microwave until warmed through, about 35 seconds. Drain the potatoes in a colander and then return to the saucepan. Mash the potatoes and then add the half and half, butter, salt, and pepper and continue to mash until smooth. Stir in the yolk until well combined.

Preheat the oven to 400° F.

While the potatoes are cooking, prepare the filling. Place the oil into a 12-inch sauté pan and set over medium-high heat. When the oil shimmers, add the onion and carrots and sauté just until they begin to take on color, approximately 3 to 4 minutes. Add the garlic and stir to combine. Add the lamb, salt and pepper and cook until browned and cooked through, approximately 3 minutes. Sprinkle the meat with the flour and toss to coat, continuing to cook for another minute. Add the tomato paste, chicken broth, Worcestershire, rosemary, thyme, and stir to combine. Bring to a boil, reduce the heat to low, cover and simmer 10 to 12 minutes or until the sauce is thickened slightly. Add the corn and peas to the lamb mixture and spread evenly into an 11 x 7-inch glass baking dish. Top with the mashed potatoes, starting around the edges to create a seal to prevent the mixture from bubbling up and smooth with a rubber spatula. Place on a parchment-lined half sheet pan on the middle rack of the oven and bake for 25 minutes or just until the potatoes begin to brown. Remove to a cooling rack for at least 15 minutes before serving.

This book is a collection of
stories centered around food, and
memories associated with various dishes.
Do you have particular likes and dislikes of food,
based on past experiences? Then you'll be able to
sympathize with the characters in these stories.

Recipes are included.

Anita Legsdin learned to cook from her mother, who learned to cook from her mother, who went to cooking school in France and became a professional chef. Of Latvian ancestry, she was indeed raised on Eastern European dishes such as sauerkraut and sausages.

www.ingramcontent.com/pod-product-compliance
Lightning Source LLC
LaVergne TN
LVHW020432080526
838202LV00055B/5155